Sonnets

Sonnets

by

Kenneth Verity

SHEPHEARD-WALWYN (PUBLISHERS) LTD

First published in 2003 by
Shepheard-Walwyn (Publishers) Ltd
Suite 604, The Chandlery
50 Westminster Bridge Road
London SE1 7QY

British Library Cataloguing in Publication Data
A catalogue record of this book
is available from the British Library

ISBN 0 85683 221 9

Typeset by Alacrity,
Banwell Castle, Weston-super-Mare
Printed through Print Solutions, Wallington, Surrey

Contents

Dedicated to

Anthony Colwell,

Publisher

About two thirds of these sonnets have been published in
two earlier collections, *The Spacious Mirror* (1973) and
The Unseen Reflection (1974), now out of print.

Author's Preface

It is said that poetry is the supreme expression of the human spirit. In substance it is an organisation and refinement of the best language with which to express human experience, making what is vital and significant in experience, permanent and memorable. Indeed, it was Keats who considered that poetry 'should strike the reader as a wording of his own highest thoughts and appear to be almost a remembrance.' Another dimension was expressed by Christopher Fry: 'Poetry is the language in which man explores his own amazement.' Poetry can, and does, intensify the sense of wonder, but only as an extension of experience and not as a substitute for it.

The poetry in this book is written as English sonnets; such a demanding and disciplined verse form was not chosen lightly. The sonnet is considered by some to be outmoded and discredited, particularly after its use by Romantics as a vehicle for dreamy, diffuse sentiment. The vigour and spare beauty of an incisively written sonnet reveals the injustice of this fusty reputation. Edward Thomas (1878-1917) wrote in a letter: 'Personally, I have a dread of the sonnet. It must contain fourteen lines and a man must be a tremendous poet or a cold mathematician if he can accommodate his thoughts to such a condition.' In my view, such a rhyming scheme is not a prescriptive tyranny; rather it is a structural matrix of benign discipline which both challenges and sustains the writer. Used adroitly, it focuses concentration and contributes to the trenchant quality which are the hallmarks of sonnet excellence.

The gradual disappearance of rhyming verse is a forfeiture of our age and its demise is an aesthetic and cultural loss. In poetry, as in anything else, mere continuance of tradition for its own sake is regressive and unjustified. But somehow we have to discover what Emerson meant when he wrote in his *Journals*: 'Poetry must be as new as foam and as old as the rock.' Writing to a structured pattern is a powerful constraint against the loose, discursive prose passing for poetry, which is shaped upon the page in order that it might merit the name poetry. Moreover, the power of the rhyme-scheme integrates the statements with an extra dimension of cohesion, rendering lines more memorable. The competence necessary for this is what constitutes the genius of a Shakespeare and the felicitous utterance of a Keats. Emerson indicated a high standard when he wrote: 'Every poem should be made up of lines that are poems.'

Much of the poetry in this volume probes deeply into the human condition with a sensitive appreciation of spiritual and aesthetic values. It has been my aim to write with an uncompromising lucidity and to offer the reader refreshment and insight.

The Renaissance poetic tradition, begun by Petrarch, evolved through the lyric writers of the Elizabethan era to reach its consummation in the genius of Shakespeare. The Elizabethan sonnet, as a verse form capable of expressing the mood and lyrical outlook of any age, has suffered undeserved neglect. The sonnets of Shakespeare (1564-1616) are an exception; they are continually accorded close attention, undergoing constant examination of sources, images and meaning. They are unsurpassed for sustained elevation and power. No selection can do justice to the impressive cumulative effect of the whole sequence. Most poets of the late 16th century were attracted by the possibilities inherent in the love sonnet and considerably extended its range. Unfortunately, they were unable to introduce a new central theme to replace the obsolete convention of courtly love. Instead, they substituted an endless repetition of sentiment and conceits which brought the sonnet into disrepute. An attempt to carry forward the development of the sonnet was made by Edmund Spenser (1552-1599), whose particular contribution was to substitute the Protestant-Platonic ideal of pure and virtuous courtship for the defunct theme of courtly love.

Most subsequent major poets have attempted to write sonnets with, it must be said, varying success. The form is at its most vital when essayed, not for academic reasons, but because it is the verse structure best suited to its theme, content and meaning.

THE FUTURE

As the 21st century begins it is accompanied by poetry – that jewel of speech almost as old as language itself. But a warning echoes from the past in the words of Macaulay: 'As civilisation advances, poetry almost necessarily declines.' These chilling words raise questions for us who write and read poetry today. Will poetry remain an apt instrument for expressing the philosophical and spiritual conceptions of mankind? Thoreau, in his *Journal*, wrote: 'Poetry implies the whole truth; philosophy expresses particles of it!' A deeper level of perception, capable of addressing truth, is possessed by metaphysical poets, but their writing is sometimes obscure. Incisive poetry which unfolds with a clear, ordered logic may yet address and reconcile the apparent difference between the ephemeral changing appearance of things and the permanent unchanging reality which supports everything. T S Eliot said: 'The poet is constantly amalgamating disparate experiences and forming new wholes.' The human being *appears* to be a divided entity, with the essential unity of nature riven, so that relationships with everything have to be formed and maintained.

There is a perceived need to make whole the self, to bring it into harmony with the total order of the Universe. To this end poetry, with its roots in experience, offers more than a furtherance of self analysis. The Elizabethan sonnet sought the re-integration of spirit and nature through the immanent alchemy of sexual love and the transcendental dynamic of personal integrity. It was also able, metaphysically, to address and touch cosmic destiny and self realisation.

In our own age, we remain held in the human predicament of an apparent separation from the unity of spirit and nature.

Yet the notional individuality of which we are so certain, is but a reflection of the ultimate oneness of an absolute being (the Universe) in which there is no separation, notional or otherwise. In order to be what we are, we have to transcend what we are not. The notional separation from the unity of everything is only a concept based on our experience of a separate physical body and social identity. Once this is realised, the perceived individuality is seen to be of a piece with the whole creation. The sonnet, with 450 years of tradition behind it, is the perfect vehicle for this philosophy.

Shakespeare addresses the beloved 'other' as himself, which he then sees everywhere:

> What is your substance, whereof are you made,
> That millions of strange shadows on you tend?
> Since every one hath, every one, one shade,
> And you but one, can every shadow lend:
>
> *Sonnet No 53*

To perceive the divine as external to ourselves is to be separate and in duality. The essential person (which embodies the divine spark) outgrows personality, becomes the self-transcendent of being and, in a likeness of unity, manifests spirit and nature as one.

After this, what of poetry and speech and words? T S Eliot gives us his answer in *Four Quartets*:

> Words, after speech, reach into the silence.
> Only by the form, the pattern,
> Can words or music reach
> The stillness, as a Chinese jar still
> Moves perpetually in its stillness.

Man and
the Natural World

The distaff of creation in the sun

A thread of substance teases out, and then

Upon the wheel of Nature's laws is spun

The universal stuff of worlds and men.

Woven upon the loom of cosmic law

Is warp and woof of all that has a place;

Whirling particles so our touch coerce

That moving points feel like a solid face.

This wondrous fabric of the universe –

Solid substance the Creator's rich store –

As finely vibrant matter makes traverse

In orbit, tracing surface evermore.

      Point, line and circle make creation's form,

      Be it a virus or a thunderstorm.

With what precision Nature shapes its course,

From tiny microbe to the distant star;

It measures out the universal force

And shapes the smallest blemish though it mar.

As water cools, the state of ice draws near;

At freezing point precisely, crystals form;

As measured moments constitute a year,

So, numbered are the raindrops in a storm.

The kestrel's plunging stoop towards the field

Unerringly secures its wriggling prey;

To growing shoot the splitting stone must yield;

The turning earth precisely marks a day:

      In all the vastness of eternal space,

      With fine exactness everything has place.

Stern Winter's frown has softened, warmth is felt,

The hand of frost retracts its icy grip;

As sunlit snow responds and starts to melt,

Icicles, moistening, slowly waste and drip.

Now shoots of green peer through the sullen ground,

Awakening life proclaims the start of Spring;

White peals of snowdrops nod in silent sound,

Catkins laden with pollen, stir and swing.

The badger snuffs abroad, his sleeping done;

Noisily, rooks repair last year's domain;

The shaky lambs stand blinking in the sun

As swelling buds first girth then colour gain.

    The sun, this season's long-awaited guest,

    Releases Nature's creatures from their rest.

As Summer brings fresh glory to the year,
Earth wears its rich luxuriance like a crown;
High overhead, from vault of heaven clear
With unrelenting eye, the sun looks down.
Cows stand in shallows at the fording place
As swans glide by, affecting cool disdain.
Swifts wheel and turn aloft with darting grace;
Haymakers toil, watchful for signs of rain.
Midst flowers in rich profusion running rife,
The droning insects work their busy day;
Some in an afternoon live out a life
The span of which a man might sleep away.

>As Summer's fruit within itself bears seeds,
>So what man does embodies future deeds.

Autumn, the consummation of the year,

When ripened fruit arches the laden bough;

With clustered nuts and standing corn's full ear

Earth's plenteousness is at the zenith now.

The spider finds upon the hedge a place

To hang a filamental mesh in air;

This retiary spinner flings a net in space

And catches drops of liquid crystal there.

The air is crisper now and, from its blue,

Creation by a gentler sun is kissed.

The bees their final garnering accrue;

At dusk the field is wet and wreathed in mist.

     Richly the Autumn crowns the year with wealth

     And, midst this plenty, time slips by in stealth.

With Winter comes the resting time of earth,

When Summer's transience withered is and lost.

Though cold and bleak this is no time of dearth,

With splendour in its guise of hoary frost.

An owl hoots eerily across the fields,

And wind moans strangely round the chimney stack;

Though dark the beauties this stark season yields,

Dull would he be of spirit who saw lack.

Frost traces ferns across the window panes,

Stealthily silent, snow drifts overnight;

Logs blaze upon the hearth, and man regains

Stored solar energy in Winter's night.

    The timely feast that marks the end of year

    Proclaims impending change, with solstice near.

Man is the measure of the universe;

The cosmic grandeur centres in his mind.

Poets proclaim its splendour with a verse,

Pointing another where to look and find.

The scupltor frees the image in the stone,

Cleaving the surplus from conceivèd form;

His feeling chisel shaping skin and bone

In more enduring substance, to inform.

The painter on his palette catches light

And with his brush to truth directs the eye,

With pigment showing us creation's flight,

Connecting mind with universals nigh.

>Reflecting back creation from the soul,

>Man lives the part relating to the whole.

Inexorably creation must unfold,

And naught can stay its urgent, stately flow.

That which is young must in its turn grow old;

All that has come will just as surely go.

The seasons move across the turning earth;

A river always flows towards the sea;

Each new beginning must embark with birth,

Come into fullness and decline to be.

Flower after flower will leave the parent corm,

Fruit follows bud, and so it thus must be;

The restless air will fulminate in storm,

Each acorn waits its chance to be a tree.

> Who tries to stem the ebb and flow of life
> Consumes his substance in a futile strife.

As mighty rock withstands th'incessant sea,

Unmoved though thunderous ocean pounds with main,

So man endures all that the fates decree,

Untouched alike by pleasure, wrath or pain.

He'll vary not as season alters ground,

Nor monthly wink as does the changeling moon;

No weathercock is he to turn him round

With each capricious breeze, like fortune's loon.

But centred firm in mind both clear and still,

His soul untrammelled by the strands of fate,

With heart embracing fortune good or ill,

He strides the moment now, inviolate.

    As truth unchanging, founded is on law,

    So man by truth surmounts each natal flaw.

The darting moorhen scuds across the lake,

Purposefully moving towards some reeds;

Her busy feet leave swirling in their wake

The water that supplies all moorhen needs.

Along the distant shore the sedge is dense,

And watchful swans nest – hid within its screen;

The stately rushes quiver, tall and tense

As tireless, lapping water chops between.

The gusty wind skimming the surface bright

Provokes to waves the water's tranquil face;

A tactile shimmer agitates the light,

Marking the wind's ephemeral swift trace.

     But as the lake is stillest where most deep,

     So I in mind's still place must watchful keep.

Our boulanger, a gastronome, has baked

A yard of golden-crusted fragrant bread.

The fingers itch as appetite is waked,

And baker's skill to hunger's need is wed.

The farmhouse brie looks cool upon the straw.

Its creamy skin yields softly to the knife;

Mature and fine, a cheese without a flaw,

Conferring credit on the farmer's wife.

The pouring wine is rising in the glass;

A burgundy of rich translucent red,

It glistens in the sunlight. Minutes pass,

The nostrils and the palate sense ahead.

>If splendour in the body's food we find,

>What shall be said of that which feeds the mind?

Untiringly the splashing fountain plays
Throughout the sultry summer afternoon.
The leaping crystal water breaks in sprays
Of sunlit rain, like liquid silver strewn.
The pool is deep beneath the lily leaves
Where, coolly, carp hide from the burning sun.
Here muted sunlight in the shadow cleaves
The green translucence where the weed is spun.
But now at dusk the busy garden rests,
The evening air is fragrant, moist and cool.
Two genial frogs, this quiet moment's guests
Sit motionless in silence by the pool.

     Water presents a simple mystery:
     How can two gases have liquidity?

In high arboreal society

To be deciduous receives acclaim,

And every truly fashionable tree

Makes change of dress each year the primal aim.

Now, as you know, we pines do not wear leaves

And sap trees tend to treat us with disdain.

Though needles lose their lustre (and this grieves)

They never rust, despite the autumn rain.

The slender straightness of the stately pine

Is envied by those trees of 'fuller shape';

And fragrant resin yielding turpentine

We think far better than a foliate cape.

     A transient outer form I rate at naught;

     The real lies deeper in, transcending thought.

Mind ponders on the force of gravity,
That constant pull towards the centre point;
Mass drawing mass in strange affinity,
Attracting by a mystery conjoint.
Since light has mass this law pervades it through,
Curving its earthward path from outer space,
Veiling what lies beyond eternal blue,
Keeping obscure creation's distant face.
But Nature's laws are everywhere the same
When from a cosmic standpoint they are seen,
And mind discovers in this lawful frame
How matter is concealed within form's screen.

    Thus gravity presents a vital fact;
    All that exists must closely interact.

A boisterous rainstorm lashed the trees last night,

The glowering sky dissolved in sheets of rain.

While crashing thunder shook the welkin height,

From heaven the pallid stars peered down in vain.

The whirling clamour moaned among the eaves;

A tile was loosed by gusts of snatching wind.

The cheerless fields were showered with falling leaves,

And ditches, choked with debris, quite o'erbrimmed.

But now at dawn, a brooding calm prevails

On aftermath of mud and broken flowers.

The sun looks down on wet dishevelled trails,

As dripping woodland drops its lesser showers.

    The summer storm, like lovers' fierce embrace,

    Anon gives way to calm, and restful peace.

The distant hills are blurred by driving rain;

A sullen peace sits broodily o'er all.

The mute bedraggled birds hide in disdain

As overhead the sky keeps spread its pall.

The plaintive calling of the sheep has ceased,

As silently across the field they pass;

So slender legged to be so heavy fleeced,

Moving in groups across the rainsoaked grass.

Two sturdy lambs, well able both to graze,

Attempt to suckle at a passing dam

But she, indignant at these outgrown ways,

Shakes herself free and butts them like a ram.

A miracle it seems of wonder full,

That fields of grass are slowly changed to wool.

Sunlight has now upon the freesias chanced

And water is to liquid crystal changed.

The flowers' rich colours are at once enhanced

As light like magic o'er their form has ranged.

The petals glisten with fine moisture's glow,

Each textured as though dusted o'er with mist;

Hued golden-yellow, paling down to snow,

The trumpets are not mute, if you but list.

They breathe a gentle fragrance fine as cloud,

Gracing the room with delicacy rare.

These lovely flowers, though splendid, are not proud;

How could they be when so discreetly fair?

    If this fine grace attends a flower's brief span,

    What follows from unfoldment of a man?

There is a language not composed of words

Spoken by waterfalls and swaying trees;

An orchestration richly voiced by birds,

Its *cantus firmus* hummed by laden bees.

A conversation sounds through nights and days

As woodland whispers, murmurs, sighs and sings;

The dripping branches punctuate the praise

Live with the vibrancy of beating wings.

Glory requires no sound to manifest,

As when the sunlight makes its arch in rain;

And craggy heights adorned with snowy crest

In silence speak their awesome message plain.

      With Nature's language only truth is heard,

      Be it an angel's voice or but a bird.

This moment poured, and waiting in the glass

Invitingly, the Mouton d'Armailhacq.

The sense of privilege begins to pass,

I raise this wine produced some decades back.

It lost its youthful purple long ago,

And now well-aged, and of a garnet hue

The edge shows some maturity; and so,

Its fragrance noted, now let taste ensue.

Silky and rich it saturates the tongue;

A shade astringent, smooth with mild decay:

Beautiful, firm – description should be sung!

The senses joy, the minutes slip away.

      Am I audacious? Must my pen malign

      In such small compass to appraise such wine?

When man looks up into the sky at night
Beyond the vastness of the Milky Way,
Towards extremity of human sight
Where only intellect can make essay;
His mind sweeps outward through the galaxy
And on where only thought can penetrate,
To meet the concept of infinity,
That all – the vast creation's correlate.
Encompassing the endlessness of space,
The countless cataclysms of the sky,
Vast tracts of aether, where in time and place,
Phenomena their meaning signify;
    Man, knowing that discernment transcends light,
    Still strives for understanding based on sight.

Plate Tectonics

Terrestrial restlessness reshapes Earth's crust,
Whose continents are awesome drifting plates
Which generate inexorable thrust
As one great mass another imbricates.
Relentlessly the movement spends its force,
Ruckling the terrain like a hilly rug;
The transform faulting at the earthquake's source
Levelling prosperous cities with a shrug.
Active volcanoes vent Earth's molten core,
Throwing out sulphur, pumice, steam and ash;
Convulsions of the shifting ocean floor
Heap tidal waves which inundate and smash.
   Thus changing geophysics leaves its trace,
   In frown and grimace on the Planet's face.

Along the rutted lane each twig and bud

Is decked with crystal beauty by the frost.

Ice-windows spanning track prints in the mud

Shatter beneath the heel, their tinkling lost

In the crunch of footsteps. Thin sunlight glows

Pale yellow through translucent mist as, down

Between the trees, it glints on winter shows

Of marble hoarfrost on primaeval brown.

Breath stabs the nostrils with a sting like knives,

Then hangs like smoke upon the freezing air;

A thrush, bold with necessity, arrives

Pleading for succour with a hungry stare.

    Creation's growth, stiffened with cold, is still;

    Held in a trance-like beauty by the chill.

Snowfall

With pressure falling and the cirrus cloud,
We recognised the harbingers of snow;
And now the racing clusters swirl and crowd
In frenzied rush to reach the earth below.
Meeting the ground the snow begins to lie,
Drifting and heaping as the blizzard grows;
The howling wind and fulminating sky
Transform the landscape into endless snows.
But now the wind has dropped, and everywhere
Familiar shapes are blurred in dazzling white;
It mutes the footfall, makes the plain seem fair,
And mantles all the countryside with light.

    Fluidity in crystal transience sleeps
    As water, in great beauty, stands in heaps.

This Earth's soft atmosphere of gracious cloud
Benignly interposed between the Sun's
Fierce heat and us, tempers with gentle shroud
The stream of fiery light which earthward runs.
Like passing thoughts, cumulus drifts across
The mind of summer's blue infinity;
Its beauty passing with no sense of loss
In skies of undisturbed serenity.
Then heavy nimbus darkly heralds change,
Muting the yellow cornfields to dull brown;
And lashing rainstorms drably disarrange
Fair summer's smiling with a thundered frown.
     With ease the sunlit play on moisture's rise
     Yields all the varied splendour of the skies.

Gone Away!

Into covert surges the eager pack;

Crispin and Prudence on the tell-tale line

Give voice, sending their rousing clamour back,

And thirty questing noses realign.

More sure and settled now, each stern[1] erect,

They work the bracken with instinctive zeal;

But though urged on by horn and voice, they've checked[2]

Where crossings[3] foil the ground and vantage steal.

Here at the corner where the coppice ends

All's still. Then something the attention grips

With that awareness when surprise impends;

And suddenly, out from the hedgerow slips

    Quite silently – escaping without rush –

    A full-grown red-brown fox with splendid brush.

1   tail
2   hounds have stopped and are casting around for a strong scent line
3   fox's trailing scent-line, criss-crosses where it doubles back on its route

A half-seen movement in the foliage

Reveals the presence of the tiny wren –

Diminutive and neat, its trim plumage

A blur of brown – now glimpsed then gone again.

Instant to instant darting, as it feeds

On tiny insects deep within the hedge;

Working the darker haunts to meet the needs

Of hungry nestlings at the meadow's edge.

Woven of moss, dead leaves and withered grass,

The snug domed nest is cleverly concealed

From those who, on the disused footpath, pass

That ivy on the wall beside the field.

    This tireless scrap of feathered energy

    Though unadorned, delights exquisitely.

Along the orchard's edge the vibrant hives

Are bristling with a seething mass of bees,

Who now at summer's height, as instinct drives,

From dawn till dusk toil at the fields and trees.

In fleeting curves they sweep to work unseen,

Then straight return with pollen-laden legs.

Deep in the darkness of the hive, their queen

With swift and silent industry lays eggs;

A realm of hexagons, a waxen world

Wrought by the architects of summer's hours,

Wherein the countless progeny lie curled,

Fragrant with propolis and juice of flowers.

　　　How much finer nectar, diligently won,

　　　Will from man's heedless spoon, as honey, run?

Ephemeral Geometrician

The skater skims the ice in gleaming arc
Poised still, in motion, on its crystal face;
This living geometry leaving scant mark,
Is executed with a dancer's grace.
A glinting blade, the flash of powdered ice
And speed is checked to make a glancing turn;
The sinewed thrust, a leap – and in a trice
Gyration blurs, beyond eyes to discern.
The forceful driving line of geese in flight,
The sweep of gulls skimming the ocean's crest,
The check of speed as waterfowl alight –
All in one motion seem to manifest.

> Movement creates a fleeting transience
> Which, as the skater rests, is lost to sense.

Double Helix

Few types of living cells are needed for

The manifold creation, which extends

From man to virus; an exterior

Which on an inward miracle depends.

The Source of Life in its artistic mode

Writes chromosomes, a choreography

Danced as mitosis. Genetic code

Creates miraculous diversity.

Deoxyribonucleic acid,

The universal molecule, convenes

Monarch and slave, and fierce or placid,

This wonderous protein constitutes their genes.

    So, Double Helix of entwinèd chain,

        Who wrote the code-script which your links
            contain?

See note 1 page 171

Haiku

Just as the snap of twigs beneath the feet,
Or the swift clean crack in a pane of glass
Hold import briefly, so may haiku greet
A flash of consciousness and mark its pass.
Seizing the instant deftly, these lines can
Catch and hold immediacy in words;
Bringing the present past, to present man
Whose mortal seconds fleet like migrant birds.
Incisive words retain the central sound,
Holding, in time, the timeless moment now;
And, stilling thoughts which mill in ceaseless round,
A transient glimpse of permanence allow.
     With the directness and the 'now' of Zen,
     The haiku speaks of truth to heedful men.

See note 2 page 171

Exploring
Metaphysics

As turning spheres mark out swift passing time

And galaxies inhale their breath of stars,

Sidereal movements arc in measured mime

As cosmic law's compulsion chance debars.

Successively each serial event

Expends, in passing, that which man calls time.

Deep in the centre naught is moved or spent,

The majesty of stillness is sublime.

If man his full affiance gave to now –

Setting invented time in lower place –

It would with joy his too-brief life endow

And give his deeds, though temporal, some grace.

    The man of spirit aeons takes as breath

    And passes through the change of birth and death.

The majesty of universal law

Confers its order on creation's span.

The scope and sweep invite a state of awe;

Its scale has power to still the breath in man.

Chance has no place within this ordered scheme,

For all its implication of caprice;

Seeming disorder is creation's stream

Slowing to entropy and full surcease.

Standpoint assigns the scale of what is seen,

For consciousness is limitless in range.

If mind can comprehend all that has been,

Knowing what is to come need not seem strange.

    The breadth of vision natural to man

      Discerns the law and does not seek a plan.

The poet's eye sweeps over Nature's span
And, resting on a detail, there reflects.
If truth enriches this perceptive scan,
What has been seen with wonder he respects.
All things which in creation move and change
Relate at source to one eternal truth;
That One, which manifests creation's range,
Is universal – though from sight aloof.
Only to insight is its face revealed,
To fine awareness in reflective mind;
When knowledge opens what before was sealed
That which had seemed so secret we may find.

    Because a point contains infinity
    We may the whole within a detail see.

When truth itself gives knowledge form, as art,

Perception is in substance manifest;

For what true artists know, that they impart

Unhampered by constraint of form's arrest.

The fire of matter is perceived by sight

As vision's percept is substantial made:

Colours express the harmony of light,

Their play on shape declared by tone and shade.

The artist shows eternity in time,

A glimpse of truth lit by his skilled address:

He draws the mind of man to the sublime

By focusing attention's restlessness.

  True art gives opportunity to find

  Communion with universal mind.

When wordlesssly creation is observed,

Each object seen is nameless – merely is.

Without the inner commentator's word

The seer sees as one all instances.

Without this verbalizing check on thought

The processing of images is swift:

Knowledge through observation comes unsought

And, hardly stirring, mind will concepts sift.

Intrinsically, the mind can operate

Without complex notations, which abound;

Only requirement to communicate

Necessitates articulated sound.

>   Words, having power to liberate or bind,
>   Inhibit thought when churning in the mind.

Meditation

As silent contemplation stills the mind,
No more is being, by the will, urged on:
Now forms and shapes no longer are defined;
The light and shadow merge, and time has gone,
Within desirelessness I am released,
Identity like some strange myth has flown;
The eye of mind is dark, all sound has ceased,
And then no thing is either heard or known ...
But consciousness returns and fills all space,
Cognition starts again where it adjourned;
The ambience resumes as time and place,
Significance and meaning have returned.

    But mind remembers its deep state of rest
    When no experience seemed manifest.

Can human minds conceive eternity,

The concept that includes and transcends time,

Envisaging what must for ever be

With no beginning, no concluding rhyme?

The mind of man expects to find a cause

For all that has occurred and is to come;

But ranging back in thought the mind will pause,

What could resource the All yet be its sum?

His contemplation finished, man can know

Creator and Creation both are one.

This wholeness with its parts will ever flow,

Always existing, boundless, not begun.

    Its total fullness cannot measured be;

    Truth, in existence *is* eternity.

Dawn

A subtle glow has lit the Eastern sky,

And night's deep shadows now prepare for flight.

We glimpse the fiery edge of heaven's eye

As earth's dark region turns into the light.

The latent forms in shadow are awake –

No longer dormant, but astir and free.

So reason permeating mind will slake

The ego's substance into nullity.

Because the earth in constant sunlight turns,

Its surface will from light to shadow move.

Because the fire of reason ever burns,

Mind's glow need not, like daylight, varying prove.

> The turning earth must brook both dark and light,
> But man has choice of mental day or night.

Pervading all that is, yet not contained,

The ever-moving Spirit free of time,

That force by which all substance is maintained,

Carrying life enters, and makes sublime.

From this potential, form can then arise,

As incremental growth begins its dance;

Function all substance shapes in fitting guise,

And so completion triumphs over chance.

The now-emergent being plays its role,

As life confers that which the form allows;

If it be man, and spirit enters soul,

Immortal will the mortal then espouse.

    Tarrying briefly, spirit rests in flesh,

    Then moving on flies free of time's brief mesh.

Meditation

Closed eyelids have the outer vision stayed,
And inner sight beholds the mind's clear ground.
Suspended are the thoughts that turmoil made;
Within this peace the stillness is profound.
The inward ear beyond the silence hears
A subtle sound that listening can refine.
In stillness now a fine cognition nears
Transcending sense, to that which is divine.
The breathing barely moves the vital air;
No image rises 'gainst the ground of thought.
Desire is dormant. I myself am there,
No longer seeking for I am the sought.

  In human form the chiefest grace is this:
  That man may know his primal state is bliss.

Emerging from Meditation

When like a deep cool lake the mind is still,

Yet to the inward eye as space is seen,

Life waits awhile; but then that space must fill.

Attention cannot stay thus held serene.

From non-cognition, mind again must know;

The outer and the inner now are two;

Attention's point is caught and tempted out,

The world of things and forms is back in view.

Mind joins again with ears and labels sounds,

The eye sees forms and mind gives each its name;

Distinctions now are drawn, so too are bounds,

All's difference now which then was all the same.

    In unity the many parts are one;

    When mind is still, diversity is none.

When is a man asleep and when awake?

And by what means may he the difference know?

How could a person dream for life mistake,

Not understanding how illusions grow?

The mind's half-waking vitiates the soul,

Discrimination is to slumber lulled,

Man's reason falters, doubted then his role;

Creation's instrument, the mind, is dulled.

Yet let this dreaming in the head but cease

And sleep be banished from the waking mind,

Then 'prisoned spirit takes its sweet release

And, soaring free, reflected truth will find.

> Then Man with bare simplicity knows this:
> His nature is truth, consciousness, and bliss.

How is it so that all-sufficient man,

To gain the pleasures loving will confer,

Disclaiming his own certain oneness can

Pretend an incompleteness without her?

Within himself man knows he is complete,

Needing no second being to be whole.

But yet he'll like some lowly creature bleat

As though he thought he had but half a soul,

Pretending to be desperate for her

And sighing low of separation's pain:

Lacking (it seems) the reason to aver

That loss of oneness, is in no sense gain.

    It seems a travesty of love to moan

      That man or woman is not whole, alone.

What is the need to worship in a man,

Making him look to power outside himself,

To which the ego, in submitting, can

With dignity surrender up its wealth?

Does deity inhabit sculptured form,

Imparting presence to a vacant shrine?

Or is it vital, free and variform,

Living in all that lives, although divine?

Let man but watch a cell divide and grow,

Or see the vital infant leave the womb;

Then may his mind an awesome wonder know,

And what is seen will inner sight illume.

    No place need be on purpose set apart

    For that which is a state of mind and heart.

Where may what is unmanifest be seen,

The point without dimension which has place?

Where else but in creation's woven screen,

Hid near, as is the self behind the face?

Unchanging always, truth remains the same,

Found close within what is in essence true.

Behind the labels, underneath the name,

From just beyond the surface truth gleams through.

The promise in the growth of sturdy youth;

The point of balance in a weighing beam;

The knowledge that attends the sound of truth;

All these reveal what may be known, not seen.

    That seen without hides what resides within:

    Look past the form and at that point begin.

Suppose the whole creation is a sound

Which man can, by audition, know in part;

If so, how do such diverse shapes abound,

And from what perfect centre does it start?

Each form in the creation rests on law,

As geometers by proposition state.

On unity the great equations draw

And universal oneness demonstrate.

Such sound as manifests is plainly heard,

But finer is the great unmanifest;

That potency pervaded by the Word

Arising from the cosmic point of rest.

    The fine elusive sound of turning spheres

    Is rather understood than heard with ears.

The strange compelling power called life is found

In all that breathes, operating unseen,

Quickening the substances that give it ground,

A living force concealed by matter's screen.

The fibre of the chromosome provides

A filamental form where, deep within,

The vital pulse of chemistry resides,

Keeping the secret of its origin.

This force which curls the tendril of the vine

Is that which pounces in the tiger's paw.

Found everywhere, its source appears divine

But veiled by seeming mystery its law.

> This is the fire that enters on a breath,

> Whose gentle exit marks what we call death.

What is the state so many fear called death,

That lonely point where life appears to cease,

When spirit's leaving ends the need for breath,

As though a tenancy had run its lease?

The lively mind's activity falls still:

Fresh genes and chromosomes its light have stored,

Passed on to children as inherent skill,

Carried as latency and held in ward.

The body's mortal function being spent,

It needs no more the form once so robust;

For, dying, we give up what life but lent,

Knowing the structure crumbles into dust.

    A flame ignites and then moves quickly on,

    The spirit enters, tarries and is gone.

When beauty's presence hovers over form
And fine delight pervades our silent awe,
Then mind may know how beauty can transform,
And how it unifies, transcending flaw.
Consonant symmetry attained by art
Cannot alone make simple objects fine;
Order and balance furnish but the start
Of what, in fullness, touches the divine.
Thus, greatness in the noble mind infers
An excellence which elevates the spirit,
And its transforming presence then confers
Immortality on earthly merit.
    Beauty arises from a state of mind
    Which, claimed and lost, leaves emptiness behind.

When harmony and counterpoint afford,

In music's concert, nourishment to mind;

When strings bowed into harmony's accord

Join instruments and voices well aligned:

These fine vibrations move the space to sound,

And ordered motion stirs the silent air;

Its measured pressures shape the aural ground,

Leaving an impress on the ambience there.

Within the milieu of the inner ear

A finer hearing answers music's voice;

Then that which seemed remote is very near

And mind's attention is a conscious choice.

      Eternal octaves all the aether fill;

      That which makes music moves, the source is still.

How patiently the turning earth bears man,

Who mars by haste, anticipating time:

That which is yet to come he tries to plan

But finds that dreams with facts will rarely chime.

Often, results are looked for in advance,

Drawing the mind from what is happening now:

Spoiling where he expected to enhance

The disillusioned man deserts the plough.

Why tear a bud, early to see its hue,

Or bite and spoil as yet unripened fruit;

Hastening a season on before 'tis due;

Urging too forwardly the eager suit?

  Each present moment holds eternity,

  And now expands if man will wait and see.

When strident claiming brashly tries to seize

What has been offered free of all reserve,

That quality which marks the mind's remise

Gently withdraws, its spirit to conserve.

Give or receive – which is transaction's shape –

And there's no need to take in earth's rich field;

Insistent laying claim is but a rape

When that which gives would rather freely yield.

Can sound be caught and held by grasping hands,

Or water be enmeshed within a net?

Man takes and his rapacity expands;

The measure being full, he wants more yet.

    A subtle greed makes simple fullness pall;

    By claiming that much more, he hazards all.

When literature, as truth, communicates
Through the aesthetic, elevating mind;
Such work the reader's knowledge illustrates,
When with his own experience aligned.
So, timelessly, great Homer draws on lore
To tell with freshness and simplicity
The epic cycle of the Trojan War,
And in the heroes we, ourselves, can see.
Then Chaucer looks on medieval man,
His eyes o'er heraldry and pilgrims range,
And in the bustle of that era's span
Again we see in men what does not change.

  But Shakespeare adds to this, in poetry,
  The potent magic of sublimity.

On steep Parnassus' flank, as though in space,

Lies Delphi razed – exposed to wind and light;

Eagles arc high above the valley's face

Circling the savage grandeur of the site.

Yet now, Apollo's oracle is still

For earth's convulsions have the chasm closed:

No more does tripod-seated priestess fill

The eager ear with rhyme in trance composed.

But though the oracle is silent now,

Truth's great injunction 'Know Thyself' yet stands;

Still the Kastalian spring's cool waters flow,

Sipped by the curious of many lands.

> Could it be yet Apollo's prompting voice
>
> When absolute detachment marks a choice?

Still arresting, there on the Argos plain,

The massy outcrop of Mycenae's stone!

Stronghold which once did all the Gulf constrain

And to whose power the Corinth route was prone.

Sombre and powerful, the Lion Gate

Leads into history and legends dim;

This timeless stone, immovable as fate,

Seems brooding, heavy – desolately grim.

Great Agamemnon's spirit haunts it still,

Mycenae's king, lord of the sea and land;

Ten years at Troy surviving every ill

Yet safely home, felled by a woman's hand.

    The sighing wind and distant goat-bells say

    Man is but mortal, brief his earthly stay.

The Parthenon set like a marble crown,

Commanding from its dais of shattered stone

The whole Acropolis, drawing renown

Upon the ageless rock which is its throne.

A hill and fortress which had been endowed

With all that men thought beautiful and fine.

Once exercised a suzerainty proud,

Whose strength is now the beauty of a shrine.

Still yet the Parthenon its grace imparts,

Those columned octaves luring wondering eyes;

Its undiminished power to hold men's hearts

Resting in what so well it sanctifies:

    Spirit of man by marble magnified,

    In this great architecture glorified!

Was Mozart born with music in his soul?

For such prodigious talent transcends blood.

Did his conceiving pre-ordain a role,

Holding impending genius in bud?

At his conception Mozart took his place;

An ovum was aroused by spirit's fire:

Such potency in such a tiny space,

A whole new sound, not uttered, yet entire.

But how was all this poised on point so fine?

Is consciousness itself impressed with form?

Heredity transmits a set design,

So does some memory new life inform?

> If genes contain the essence of the whole,
>
> What causal agent shines within a soul?

Too often blind belief obscures the truth,

Closing the mind to what creation is;

It makes the superstitious yearn for proof

And feel impelled to search out instances.

By contrast, if man's trust resides in law

Where permanence survives creation's flight,

Each inference he may with sureness draw

From observation made in reason's light.

With reason's entry knowledge may arise

As trust compels emotion to subside;

And truth, which wears existence as a guise,

Will be perceived in substance to reside.

> Man's faith provides that subtle chemistry
>
> Which stills the mind by setting spirit free.

Leonardo da Vinci

A giant in an age of mighty men,
Who read the realm of nature as his book;
Whose scalpel, sculptor's chisel, brush and pen
Showed other men how he instruction took.
What he discerned in nature, that he taught,
Who in a corpse could living knowledge find:
There in the manuscripts is what he thought
Whose work endures – the mirror of his mind.
Perhaps his Mona Lisa stands supreme,
Still vital with serene seductive grace;
Whose lineaments four years of toil redeem
As genius distilled within a face.

     Great master of the art concealing art,
     Who in a whole renaissance stands apart!

Full justice reigns in universal law

Where all is one and everything is free:

Throughout creation only man sees flaw,

Whose acts so often flout that law's decree.

All natural law must act impartially –

As water in free state must downward flow:

No one seeks favours from the mighty sea;

And life itself departs when law says 'Go'!

Justice will never take a partial view

For it is measured, whole and absolute:

A concept firmly based on one, not two,

And being constant it does not commute.

      When truth pervades the mind and life of man,

      Then universal justice fills his scan.

The wraith-like fears that lurk within the mind

Are less substantial than the clouds in air;

Seek them with reason's eye and you will find

A vanished predator, an empty lair.

So what creates the gnawing doubts and pain,

The irksome apprehensions men endure;

Who miser-like compute their loss and gain,

Hesitant to give; dubious, unsure?

Fear is the consequential mental state

That follows on a fall from unity;

And this division, with its fear of fate,

Leads to increasing subjectivity.

> Where doubt divides – there reason soon resolves:
> Establish unity and fear dissolves.

The living stone of Chartres cathedral sings,
Its massive finely carved exterior
A rich magnificence, from which there springs
The soundless praise of a vast sculptured choir!
Within, the vibrant living atmosphere
Remains serene as generations pass;
The subtle muted light is strangely clear,
Tinged with the fire of multi-coloured glass.
The flying buttresses, absorbing thrust,
Allow an unencumbered inner space;
A calming stillness men can feel and trust –
The rich experience of present grace.

  Fired with the impulse which produced this shrine
  Man's soaring spirit touches the divine.

I sit in meditation – thought has ceased;

The growing silence deepens under will;

Discursive mental pressures are released

And mind is centred, wide awake and still.

Inner responses cease their constant play

As each disturbance yields to will's fine force;

All trace of movement gently ebbs away

As what is cognate turns towards its source.

Direction lies beyond what is unknown,

The darkness is translucent clear and full;

Subject and object disappear in one;

Being is fully present, and is all.

    At this, experience recedes in rest

    And what I knew, no more is manifest.

Existence is beyond the reach of thought,

Yet may be found as close as life itself.

It silently recedes if it is sought,

But man pursues it with his spirit's wealth.

Hunting outside for that which lies within,

Or seeking inward what is everywhere;

Men chase existence as a prize to win,

As if to be what is, were something rare.

This threshold though unseen is very near,

Crossed as a simple step within the mind;

That which is present is both now and here;

Only as searching ceases will man find.

When mind no more divides 'I am' from 'me'.

Then is existence just the verb to be.

The world is an illusion say the wise,

And what we see just transitory change;

That which is real is not observed with eyes

For truth is veiled throughout the senses' range.

If things perceived are not what they appear,

The form and surface fading, as do dreams;

Then what is vital must be very near,

Its presence closer than at first it seems.

Though outer shapes conceal the real within,

And grosser substance finer substance hides,

That point from which things manifest begin –

The truth itself – in everything resides!

    Mistake appearance for entirety

    And all creation is illusory.

Perfection as a concept limits man,

That which is faultless lives but in the mind:

For where in all creation's myriad span

Is flawlessness to transience assigned?

Except in mind there is no perfect shape,

In Nature's realm straight lines do not exist.

How often do we find a spheric grape?

When twins are born, is this perfection missed?

If man were free to change what he thinks mars,

Suppressing 'evil' and promoting 'good',

His prejudice would reach the very stars

And could he alter Nature's laws, he would.

      Not by excluding is the perfect gained,

      But with inclusion wholeness is sustained.

One spirit animates the lives of all,

But what this means, man hardly comprehends,

With life's potential made the body's thrall,

No further than the skin his 'I' extends.

Dulled in perception man the real negates,

Dreaming, imprisoned in his mental cell;

Projecting with the mind, he then creates

A private universe in which to dwell.

The mere conferring of a separate name

Does not, *per se*, discrete existence give.

Each entity in essence is the same,

Each man, spirit choosing in flesh to live.

> Appearances are not what they may seem:
> When one is seen as many, we but dream.

See how the glory emanates from Sun,

The great star's radiance by which all see!

A vast outpouring (in which Earth is spun)

Of warming light and vital energy.

It fills the clear discerning eye of man

Illuminating everything observed;

Pervading too the intervening span,

One light lights all, and oneness is conserved.

Blazing as comprehension, it sets free

The clear discrimination of the mind;

Lit with this insight inner eye can see,

And with discernment understanding find.

       Then as creation's splendour fills man's sight

       He sees its glory as the spirit's light.

Stemming from truth, I am by that name called

Back to the source which gave this substance life.

I am, as living spirit, fleshly walled

Yet free of confines and emotion's strife.

Moving through Nature, spirit holds its course

Journeying on from life to life, still free;

Constantly felt as will's compelling force,

Glimpsed in the mind where inner eye can see.

Spirit, like flame, gives light as it consumes –

As substance burns the life gains means to be.

Form after form the spirit re-assumes,

Causeless, eternal, ever new and free.

> What force makes spirit turn again to earth?

> What lingers after life, re-seeking birth?

To the Heavenly Firebringer

Prometheus! bringer of fire to men,
Who for that act endured the wrath of Zeus –
Know that ignition, vital now as then,
Has been from all constraint by men prised loose.
For now is gone the frenzied rub of wood,
The precious tinder-box and fiery flint;
Our sulphurous matches now are very good,
And ways to tap the sun itself we mint!
What have we done with this your wondrous gift
Except replace sun's heat when winter's here?
Well, gunpowder has caused its share of rift
And, sadly, mushroom-clouds give rise to fear;
    But keep your faith in us, fire-bringing god;
    Your gift is still a staff more than a rod.

The cosmic potter spins this earthly wheel,

His mighty kiln the ever-burning sun.

Mountains and seas his awesome power reveal,

Yet that same hand the spider's web has spun.

He curved with ease the azure bowl above,

Lifting the hills and spreading plains below;

Shaping this rich creation with a love

Which man feels in his own creative flow.

The laden clouds like pitchers spilling rain

Augment the ocean; which when warmed by sun,

And rising, forms the misty clouds again

As moisture must its wonderous circle run.

    Frail earthen vessels shaped by mighty force,

    Look past the clay-wrought splendour to the source!

Meditation

Seated and still – within myself the guest,
Both hemispheres of mind in equipoise;
Reason and intellect are now at rest,
For no event discernment's eye employs.
No inner voice speaks words and sentences
In commentary on what the sense has caught;
That which I felt I was, no longer is;
Such dreamed existence was a toy of thought.
Life is perceived to be a pulsing stream –
Phenomena, of passing movement spun.
All that was sensed before now seems a dream;
Plurality has been absorbed in one.

      Spirit, untrammelled by creation's thrall
        Is, in this timelessness, acknowledged All.

Chinese Porcelain

When fire combines as one the properties
Of kaolin and feldspar; pot and glaze
Fuse as a unity, whose qualities
Of thin translucent resonance amaze.
The chiming music of Sung, Ch'ing, Ming, T'ang,
Proclaim dynastic China's porcelain:
Ceramics yielding still the sound that rang
In ear of emperor and mandarin.
The eye of mind, perceiving form, discerns
In Sung an understated elegance;
And from this clear serenity, it turns
To Ming – resplendent in its arrogance.
    This clay, symbol of man's mortality,
    Brittle but splendid in finality.

Gods and Heroes

Some men like giants have bestridden time,

Their splendid deeds by legend magnified;

Whose exploits brought them fame beyond their clime;

Who were an archetype exemplified.

Such was great Heracles, a man of fate

Whose floruit fore-ran the Trojan War;

A man of certain ancestry and date,

Whose 'Labours' constitute his legend's core.

Asklepios: physician, man and myth;

To whom in time a hero cult attached,

He too was deified, and was forthwith

Quite from his mortal history detached.

> If men with human form their gods invest,
>
> Their heroes soon, as gods, will manifest.

Lignum Vitae

More logs are thrust into the flickering glare,

The blazing fire adjusts with crack and spark;

And though at first no sign arises there,

A curl of smoke now stirs beneath the bark.

Then, as the wood aggressed by eager fire

Glows with an incandescence like the sun,

The heat consumes it like a fierce desire

As unchecked energies abandoned run.

Later, the blazing hearth is not so brash,

The fire begins to settle and die low;

Remains of logs slump in the silvery ash,

Suffusing sense benignly with their glow.

    Like trees, we men which long in sunlight stood,

    Must yield what we were lent as growing wood.

Meditation

I sit in silence, disengaged from quest,
Life's energies are cooled to heatless fire;
With balance now restored, and deep in rest,
The consciousness is emptied of desire.
All that was once imagined has dissolved,
A merging integrates the separateness;
Apparent difference has been resolved
And urgent passing time hangs motionless.
No voluntary action has support,
The body image held in mind has gone;
There is no need to shape or frame a thought,
Nothing remains to make comparison.

    In spacious stillness, yielding all reserve;
    As the eternal witness, I observe.

Encounter with a Kore (Acropolis Museum)

A fleeting time transcendence in the mind,

A glance which penetrates the surface form

And suddenly, life seems to breathe behind

The marble smile. Thus may a look transform!

This miracle, combining sculptors' skill

(Who carved a softness into lifeless stone)

With Nature's art: which wrought those curves that still

Enchant our eyes, transcending skill alone.

Her stony mantle, ever still, yet stirs

With youthful fire and graciousness of soul;

And guilelessly her countenance avers

That manifesting Truth is beauty's role.

For in the haunting beauty of her smile

The Grecian spirit lingers all this while.

See note 3 page 171

Erotic Spirituality – The Temples at Khajuraho

Articulate sandstone, the ravages

Of blurring wind and time have failed to mute

Your song, have not yet quelled your images,

Which with their praises joyfully refute

The *gravitas* that mars philosophy.

Your gracefully inflected sculptures sing

Of the creation's deepest mystery.

Unstraitened, and in its joy delighting,

The Cosmic Principals conjoin to show

Essence and Substance merged as one, in this

Portrayal of creation's play – whence flow

Sublime delight and universal bliss.

>   As mind transcends all concepts and is free,

>   It mirrors all that is, in unity.

See note 4 page 171

Tao

What is the eternal changeless Tao,

The nameless ultimate reality;

Which, measureless untouchable, is now,

That ears hear not, and mens' eyes cannot see?

Life's everchanging flow, the surging growth

Itself, though moved by Tao, cannot contain

Undifferentiated wholeness; both

Must pass, but space and Tao remain.

The sages find in Tao their resting place,

Where emptied, and with earnest seeking done,

They penetrate the absolute of space

And ask not, 'What is Tao or what is One?'

> For he who knows it not, is he who speaks;
>
> But one who truly knows, his silence keeps.

See note 5 page 172

Jalal al-Din Rūmī

Great mystic poet, born at Khorasan,
Who heard the plaintive singing of the reed
Yearning for its return to source; each man
Once emptied of himself has known this need.
Great master-teacher of the truth, who taught
A Way which makes the oneness actual;
In Konya, still revered as he who wrought
The Mevlevi's inspiring ritual.
Serenely, as the whirling dervishes
Turning about an inner stillness, spin;
Their motion, of itself, establishes
That movement rests on changeless truth within.
> Rūmī, your lyric verse and dance express
> The ecstasy of single-mindedness!

See note 6 page 172

Monteverdi

Cremona's noblest son, your skills caress
The aether into audibility!
Who does with music straight our soul address,
Drawing the mind to inner unity;
Who with consummate mastery composed
Eight books of madrigals on love and war;
Whose operas and masses so disposed
Their hearers as to make discernment soar.
Music reflecting meaning, word by word;
Humour and drama, jealousy and love:
Such aural splendours that we, having heard,
Feel spirit deep within our being move.

> You who were, while living, respected so
> That you were called 'Divino Claudio'!

Plato's World of Forms

Plato contended that Ideas exist

Quite independently of mind and things.

If so where do they live; on what subsist?

And what the ground from which a concept springs?

Its milieu is accessible to mind,

The stream of discourse is its ebb and flow;

And use of reason is the way to find

That inner resonance which is, 'to know'.

Truth draws the reason to reality,

To permanence behind the flux of change;

And in the light of actuality,

Our questing thought transcends its finite range.

    All worlds connect and everywhere begin;

    Mind's inspiration comes with breathing in.

Utamaro

How deftly, and with what a simple line
The skilful brush of Utamaro spans
A varied world. In delicate design
The insects, birds, lovers and courtesans
He saw, still live in timeless colour prints.
With brilliant technical resource, he gives
Micaceous sheen to wings; in hues and tints
The iridescence in a snail's shell lives.
Those ladies too, mannered but exquisite,
So much enjoying Sumida River,
Glow in their portraits; their vanished world – lit
By this vital brush – endures for ever.
    This master of his genre, holds his place
    Among the best who moved a line through space.

See note 7 page 172

Harrow Hill

Upraised before recorded history,
The lofty summit of this ageless hill
Has been a vantage point for centuries
For Saxons, kings – and we who walk here still.
Its verdant shoulders graciously have borne
Old Lanfranc's church and good John Lyon's school;
Its winding streets and canting road well worn
By journeyings both grand and minescule.
How many boys reached manhood on its back,
Gazing out worldward from its gentle height?
What deeds they did – for none did courage lack,
These sons of Harrow in their glory's flight!
     Beneath the public school and churchyard stones,
     The Hill stands firm and great renown enthrones.

Communication

The publisher presents to all who read
What his discrimination marks as fine;
And through the permanence of print sows seed
Which yields its harvest in a distant time.
Thus books enable men long dead to speak
To others breathing still; through print we find
A living scholar and an ancient Greek
Communing in the timelessness of mind.
A book's creator as he works for Man
Will like a lapidary both incise
And polish, that the outcome which we scan
May as it pleases mind, delight the eyes.

What men have valued they have widely spread;
Unpublished, might a Plato go unread?

Seeking the Meaning of Christmas

If in the Christmas stillness man should pause,

With reason penetrating mystery,

To him the virgin-born says, 'Without cause

And ere earth was, I am – return to Me.'

The manger beasts placed near at this event

Sense in simplicity and patient stand.

Not so the Magi, marking heav'ns portent,

Are moving lightward through the sleeping land.

May our discernment see behind the flesh

With virginal potential to receive;

May spirit penetrate the mind afresh

That we, with open hearts, might Truth conceive.

    Come sleep-dispelling sun, thou Son of Light

    Divinely visit man, dispel mind's night!

De Nativitate Domini

Serene, a star gleams high above the night
Which shrouds mankind in darkness of the mind:
And, in the stillness, waits the source of light
That three wise men have come so far to find.
In mystery, born as a virgin's son,
Earth's maker is His own creation's guest;
Now consciousness conceives that All is One
For God and Man within one cradle rest.
A wondrous interchange by this is wrought
As flesh becomes the vehicle of God;
The absolute creative power has sought
To walk, Himself, the path which Man has trod:
  And gracing virgin receptivity
  Immanent God incurs nativity!

Grammar of the Universe

This wondrous universe, this predicate,
Proclaims its subject – spirit manifest;
The pronoun Trinity some designate
First Person, Middle Person and the Best.
The ultimate collective noun is One,
Its verbal being, 'I am That', the All
Arisen in Creation. It has spun
A syntax out of which we disenthral
That single verb which, as the active voice,
First spoke the genitive imperative.
Can any adjective of human choice
Augment the cosmic nominative?
　　　Divine Grammarian who made the stars,
　　　Inspire our reason, as in awe, we parse.

Retrospection Occasioned by a Photograph

At fifteen years the eyes are clear and still,
The brow untroubled and the mouth serene;
Evincing mildness and a passive will,
A child who has as yet no sorrow seen.
Large eyed, attractive with a simple grace,
The flower of womanhood, in bud as yet;
Devoid of guile, this gentle open face
Shows outwardly how what is inward set.
Here in this child, vital with ready verve,
The innocence and loveliness converge;
Willing, obedient and prepared to serve,
The woman hovers waiting to emerge.
    This gentle dawn suggests a beauteous day,
    And what she is will both remain – and stay.

The Vanity of Enforced Belief

How many men who died for blind belief
Now lie dissolved within the wastes of time?
What took their life like some o'er-hasty thief,
Making 'belief' excuse for heinous crime?
Vast numbers died to prove what they believed,
A vital gesture made with dying breath;
But ignorance their torturer's mind deceived,
How could it serve the truth, this feast of death?
On such a diet Torquemada thrived,
Crushing men's bodies to release the soul:
Mere crimes of ego at which popes connived,
And forcing mere belief was all their goal.
    Belief is but a substitute for truth,
    As faith awaits that knowledge some call proof.

The Anger of Morality

There is an anger in morality,
Which seems to stem from some untruth within
The self-styled agents of the Deity,
Who claim they know what constitutes a sin.
For morals differ with locality,
And ethnic variations indicate
That often, artificiality
Was formalized and then made consecrate.
The universals in the life of man,
In correspondence with the cosmic laws,
Are not contained within our morals' span –
The neutral truth no bounds of conduct draws.
    Truth is eternal; morals have their mode,
    But anger points to ego in the code.

The Lust for Certainty

Must all philosophies and faiths assert
That each alone expounds with certitude
Creation's secrets and, what's more, dissert
What is averred with cant and sanctitude?
This vehemence reveals much hint of doubt
Suppressed, for careful questioning is met
By endless reassertions, some devout
But others with strong prejudice beset.
For as usurping lust employs duress
To seize what it cannot by love obtain;
So those who lust for certitude repress
Pursuit of truth itself – for ego's gain.
      No mode of thought has yet, or ever can
      Bring total certainty to mind of man.

The Greed for Piety

In some there is a greed for piety
Which seems at source to be a fear of life;
This pietism – false propriety –
Sets mind at body in a constant strife.
Yet since the body is controlled by mind,
Should it be punished for the mind's default?
That tortured instrument repays in kind,
And visits back unreasonable assault.
Life's gift is not a punishment for sin
In creatures constantly conceiving ill;
Man has within himself a discipline,
Founded on reason and the power of will.
    Can we our maker bribe with sacrifice,
    Or is requital, truth for Truth, His price?

Doctor Faustus

Wittenberg's Faustus brooding on his books,
Searches his academic emptiness
For life and, *in extremis*, turns and looks
To evil for renewed creativeness.
The play of Marlowe vividly describes
The grave disintegration of a man
Who, his eternal freedom circumscribes,
For brief extension of his earthly span.
The playwright, in the figure of his age,
Depicts a man spurning his destined role:
Powers of light and darkness walk the stage;
Faustus, by deed-of-blood, yields up his soul.

    'Hell strives with grace for conquest in his breast.'
    Does any man, ere death, escape this test?

The Numinous

How full the silence is and deeply still,

Yet palpable within the listening ear;

Which does, as presence, all the cosmos fill,

The immanent sustaining power – is near.

Not temporal, yet realizable

Within the moment of immediacy;

Inapprehensible, unnameable,

Mysterious transcendent unity.

Outsoaring all conception of the mind,

Incomprehensible to human thought;

Direct perception opens and we find

What would not manifest while being sought.

    It waits until, in stillness, we address

    The immanent indwelling consciousness.

Persian Carpets

There in Tabriz, Saruk and Khorasan,
Where life is time spent crouched before the loom;
Nimble brown fingers work the knotted span
That spreads its richness in the dreary room.
The wrinkled elders teach their ancient skill
To children who will into carpets grow;
Who sit with lively limbs cramped close and still
As time ekes out its patterned woven flow.
Forth from the dingy workshops of the East
Where village people their fulfilment find,
Carpets for prayer and rugs to grace the feast,
In strange designs which satisfy the mind

    Pass 'neath the grasping merchant's eager scan,
    There in Tabriz, Saruk and Khorasan.

Just a Moment

The present moment, joining now with here,
Strangely co-ordinates all time and space;
A point amid events in full career
Which, in the vastness, specifies this place.
Ever outside the time devised by man,
With its fixed intervals and constant change;
Here now but ever yet, the moment's span
Remains the present through succession's range.
This vibrancy, on passing through the sun,
Measures the life of all within that light;
It body's forth, maintains and ends the run
Of all not deemed eternal in its sight.

    The past is gone, the future yet to be;
    But both exist as 'now' alive in me.

Poetry

In mind where images and echoes throng,
The poet heeds the muse's prompting voice;
And in the measures of iambic song
Echoes the harmony he hears by choice.
For in the dissonance of earthly din
Resounds the canticle of excellence;
Supernal beauty is reflected in
The images and shadows caught by sense.
Then spirit soars as if in angel's flight,
The purely excellent is known to be;
And thus informed by grace the inner sight
Perceives a universal harmony;

    With sounds and measures of his potent art
    The poet strives his vision to impart.

The Nature
of Love

Breaking from covert on the path ahead,

A stag in silent majesty goes by.

Of airy lightness seems the antler spread,

So nobly is it borne against the sky.

He stands quite still, beneath a massive tree

Whose mighty boughs spread darkly low and wide,

And views his verdant terrain. Wild and free

He waits, a living challenge bold with pride.

Close by, the gentle does lie grouped at peace;

Their spotted backs just break above the grass.

All's still; even the wind's slight movements cease

As, rich with sylvan splendour, minutes pass.

> We drink this scene together you and I,
>
> Not two but one in love's sweet company.

Aurora rises russet-clad from night,

And gloriously begins another day.

The eastern sky is touched with wakening light

As night's dark mantle gently falls away.

The welkin sings as birds pour out their lays

Of liquid piping to the sun's rich fire.

The solar splendour lifts man's heart to praise;

All substance sings in universal choir.

Ever from boundless azure heav'ns eye burns,

Vivifying earth with life-conferring rays.

My love to you so radiantly returns,

That like a second sun you light my days.

    Sun's splendour crowns the zenith of the morn

    As you, rich jewel, my earthly life adorn.

As gentle rain brings nourishment to earth,

Conferring rich abundance from above,

So woman's nature brings man's joy to birth

When graciously she gives to him her love.

With countenance reflecting inner joy,

Her comely mien on all bestowing light,

Delighted is she if without alloy

Her service is full pleasing in his sight.

As bounteous Nature gives from her full store

Without reserve, offering rich expense,

The woman's grace enhancèd is the more

If rousing love she too delights the sense.

    As splendour crowns the sun's enlivening rays,

    So woman glorifies man's earthly days.

When I recall within my heart your voice,
Hearing again the dearest sound I know,
Of all the treasured aural realm my choice
Is hearing you confess your love will grow.
No metal-hearted bell with iron tongue
Nor bird's thin pipe could ever match the grace
With which your phrases on the air are hung,
Each arching cadence leaving fleeting trace.
The very sighs come singing from your breast:
Consummate artistry so crowns your speech
Its sonant phrases lull my ears to rest,
As soul and soul does each to other reach.
     Though hearing finds such treasure in each sound,
     Within the silence love is most profound.

How can mere eyes alone appraise your worth

When outer shapes and forms are all their view?

A single sense could yield naught else but dearth,

Unless the being practised loving you.

The eye rests on appearances alone

But true perception penetrates beyond.

As your rich love exceeds all I had known

So I, in turn, with my whole self respond.

The source of all my joy springs from your heart

And praise of you is my outgoing breath.

Your love does very life to me impart;

Withdraw it, and you sentence me to death.

    Although my eyes discern a maiden's shell,

    Surely within, an angel there must dwell?

A silver lantern in the heavens is hung,

The crescent bow set high above the trees;

Its arching radiance into space is sung

And by its gentle light the lover sees.

Bright stars the luminescent heav'ns adorn,

The moonlit dew lies glistening on the grass;

So fleeting hours of night that speed t'ward dawn

Are touched with lustrous beauty as they pass.

But, splendid as these jewels of night may seem,

Your richness, dearest, far surpasses all;

For stars dance in your smile, your bright eyes gleam,

Before your grace the moon's pale light must pall.

　　Moon gives its splendour only to the night,

　　But you exalt creation by your light.

What is it you confer, what quality,

That renders simple things more richly full;

Not impairing the root simplicity

And yet, enhancing like a flame, its fuel?

Your joy in all that you both hear and see,

The quick delight in beauty everywhere;

These give a richness to your company,

Making the shared things seem more fine and rare.

You are a banquet surfeit cannot pall,

Though rich the fare when you are in that guise.

If you should hear me say my fortunes fall,

Vouchsafe me glimpses from those jewels your eyes.

     Unlid your treasure dearest, look this way

     And I shall feast on stars though it be day.

Two hearts in love may consonantly beat

As though both live within a single breast;

And yet still is this concord incomplete

If minds are not, like hearts, with love impressed.

It needs no band of gold upon the hand

To symbolise two minds in full accord;

For where two streams in confluence sweep the strand

By joinèd fullness is their course assured.

As moving notes traverse an ordered ground,

Tracing out music's flow in measured line,

So two in love produce accordant sound

As they, with joy, their separateness resign.

    For when love's two serve one in harmony

    Then are they both conjoined in symmetry.

In memory I summon up your face

And in its features read love written there.

My heart rejoices to recall your grace,

For joy's enthronement exiles gloom and care.

Your ringing laughter is the silver sound

Whose music finds the ear within my heart.

Remembrance then with harmony is crowned –

Adding to inner sight its aural part.

When you are speaking, love attunes my ears,

For that dear voice a yearning satisfies;

And in your speech it joyfully appears

The words but echo what is in your eyes.

    If you make music just by speaking words,

    O do not sing or you will quiet the birds.

I sometimes wonder at your love for me;

Yet, why should I expect you to explain?

Must flowers their fragrance justify by plea,

Or clouds give reasons when they drop the rain?

The sun before it warms does not seek leave,

Nor sky give explanation of its blue.

No more of questions that composure cleave,

But how to love you more, that I'll construe.

Love will those things we value finely sift,

And I respond with what is best in me.

When life itself is all Creation's gift,

Could I withhold a love already free?

>As much as I give you from my full store
>So I receive, which makes it thus the more.

Come do not weep my love, not e'en for joy,

Lest with your lids your spirit too decline;

But let the heart some other means employ

To give the inward melting outward sign.

The liquid pearls that dew those lovely eyes

Are costly beads I do not joy to view.

Though valued more than oyster's hidden prize,

Their price too dear if bought of pain in you.

Have done with tears, and let this April grow

To June; that smilingly, new-clothed with love,

The inner radiance making outward show,

To all the world your love's effect you'll prove.

  If I may grace confer where once was pain,

  Then are we blest, and all mankind will gain.

Is it your muse I love so well, or you?

I ask this question, hoping you may then,

While so engaged, be less inclined to rue

The paler work created by my pen.

Maids not so gifted wag their tongues in prose,

But you my love, in sonnets speak your heart;

And just as fragrance does not make the rose,

So poesy is not your better part.

Know that I love you for your gracious self,

And, though your gift has earned my high esteem,

Within your gentle heart lies all my wealth;

And if you could not write still rich you'd seem.

    To praise your skill I too have taken pen,

    And while I breathe it shall not rest again.

Innocence like a fragrance graces you

And makes of you the flower of beauty's field.

Why seem you so surprised that I pursue

The rare delight which you in presence yield?

My soul is winnowed by your zephyr sighs

In seeming endless flow from love's rich store.

No aspen stirred as summer's breezes rise

Could ever be as odorously breathed o'er.

The air inspired by you has life the more,

Made redolent of your intrinsic worth;

Your outward breaths my inward life restore,

Giving thereby my poetry its birth.

    As flowers yield fragrant treasure to the bee,

    So you bestow preferment upon me.

When in the earth your body sleeps in death

And your sweet soul has through the aether sped,

That quick spirit flown on departed breath

And the fire cooled which your heart's warmth once fed;

When your dear voice no more shall grace the air

And sense is dulled by Death's consuming rust,

When those bright eyes are closed to all that's fair,

Those rills of laughter choked with dateless dust;

This sad description shall not be your end:

For your dear presence shall by men be known

Yet living in the words which I have penned;

Your grace in stanzas will to all be shown.

> While men still read, these words which sing your
> praise
>
> Shall give you life beyond your span of days.

When Nature poured on you felicity,

Bestowing such full treasure on one soul;

Potential spoke, and you were its decree:

Creation's focus on the woman's role.

The tender qualities in you denote

A rich excelling of your kind in grace,

And any fault appears but as a mote

That might dance lightly on a sunbeam's face.

And yet my eyes wink not, they plainly view,

All that is there I can behold;

But O, your grace such richness gives to you

As when the sunlight bathes a scene with gold.

     Illusion need not rise in front of me

     With so much splendour in reality.

My tongue falls silent, quietly resigned

Within the lovely margent of your kiss,

And magically from our two tongues combined

The alchemy of taste compounds its bliss.

Like stately progress of some special feast,

Your kisses grow in richness by the hour.

Desire does not diminish in the least

But rather is enhancèd by their power.

Although my tongue could give a soft caress,

Its impish probing seeks to stir you much;

So use your own, approve this dear duress,

And to the joy of taste let tongue add touch,

    Although your speech delights, O love make haste!

    Let words be still while I your kisses taste.

When words have ceased and sighs disturb the calm
And orchestrated hands begin their play,
Then brings the sense of touch its gentle balm,
Soothing sweet aches and yearning's pain away.
Entwinèd arms in rich embracement give
Their ardent reassuring pledge of love.
With cadences of touch the moments live;
In tactile harmony the minutes move;
Caressing hands in silent message speak
And full response appears to need no rest.
Sweet searching fingers find the place they seek
And yearning flesh by love's sweet salve is blest.

  Yet body's touch plays but an outward part:
  It is with love that we caress the heart.

When you gave upward glance toward the stairs
And winged your love to me-ward with a look,
That moment's joy dissolved the world's affairs
And time its urgency and pace forsook.
Now, just as then, we both our gaze assign
And eyes again in wrapt engagement meet;
The wealth within your heart you change for mine,
As passing moment waits while two souls greet.
Inward embracement starts with outer forms,
But surging alchemy its fire imparts,
The pales of shy reserve are quickly stormed
And oneness is, where formerly were parts.

      As giving soars, sweeping to summit's height,
      Experience translates to sheer delight.

Dear one, how could your value measured be,

Who for so long my every need has met,

Giving without reserve your company

When I have been with pressing care beset?

So natural I find your comely grace,

Your willingness to give with all your heart,

That those days spent in your sweet care I place

In memory's special seat, quite set apart.

And too, so wholly woman are you made

That joy of you 'tis privilege to take.

All I give you most fully is repaid,

So rich the service offered for my sake.

As you have taught me how to love and give,

I will them both requite while I do live.

When I a man step down from unity
To feel a need most satisfied by you,
I know that pangs attend duality
That separation can arise with two.
Yet, complementing this, you in like case
Leave that same unity which is your own;
And as I look upon your joyful face
Clearly no sense of loss by you is known.
A quality stemming from inward grace
Flows from your being as a radiant light.
Self, which I clearly see within your face,
Shines, as the brightness of the sun to sight.

    Oneness of life pervades the human heart;
    Each in the other lives, neither apart.

The hurrying water chuckles over stones,

And cascades glistening at the weir's edge;

The river's gurgling merriment atones

For torpid gloom beneath the rush and sedge.

The skies of April are but briefly grey,

So swiftly pass the clouds and drenching showers;

And soon in benediction comes the sun

To smile on burgeoning trees and fragrant flowers.

Creation's joy is not concealed from eyes

But, like your love, apparent on its face;

And as the Spring earth's visage beautifies,

So does your smile enhance an inward grace.

    Where your fresh laughter dances on the air,

    Felicity proclaims your presence there.

The fragrant mantle man has named the earth,

That first receives then cradles every seed,

This teeming womb that gives all life its birth

Is ever fruitful, ever meeting need.

The velvet mole that delves beneath the field,

The patient cattle grazing by the hour,

The tugging thrush to which the worm must yield;

Each to its larder turns, and sups its power.

The changing seasons husband well the soil,

Bringing deep warmth and penetrating rain.

Clod-breaking frost abates man's earthly toil,

And all conjoined achieve a mutual gain.

    As earth's rich substance ever offers place,

    So woman unto man yields her embrace.

Do any doubt that sentiment will kill,

As surely as the spider drains the fly?

Relationships so tainted, must and will

Disintegrate within, and slowly die.

Sentiment takes, by a pretence to give,

Laying a facile gloss on life's true face.

In such an atmosphere love cannot live

But, suffocating, dies for want of grace.

The heart's effusive gush needs reason's check

If truth's reflection is what would be found;

This helmsman saves emotion's barque from wreck,

Which otherwise in dreams will run aground.

    Unless as one the heart and mind engage,

    The cloy of sentiment will grow with age.

Does man too readily consider Love
A synonym for life's maintaining force;
As though it stayed the firmament above,
Holding the spinning planets in their course?
A bird will yield its life to save its brood,
And human parents match this costly care,
The powerful instinct Nature has imbued
Makes such a sacrifice by no means rare.
Yet man looks further than his human life,
Having in stewardship the earth's rich store;
Above his outer wars and inner strife
There operates for him a higher law.

    A simple act puts instinct under grace
    Before oneself, to give another place.

You are no actress playing out a part;

Brushing the simulated tear away,

Averting eyes to show a wounded heart,

Speaking your lines to see what people say.

Nor do you cull some minor poet's verse

To give obscure emotions vague account,

And with this prop – a trick or two perverse

Present a dream – or me you'd quite miscount.

You are direct and what you are we see

Clearly alight and shining in your face,

And when you speak both heart and mind agree

Life is too short to give our dreams a place.

If in this lifetime loving is our task,

Waste not one hour behind an actress' mask!

Seeing these clustered hazels on the bough
Plump round and full, the hedgerow's shy surprise;
I muse upon the chance that could allow
Their name to be the colour of your eyes.
Within those lustrous orbs my sun resides,
All's night when in your sleep their light is sealed;
But with the dawn each curving fringe divides
And in a look your radiance is revealed.
By depth of fullness love can measured be,
And your dark eyes an ocean's deepness hold;
Yet such rich wealth the main will never see
For all its argosies of sunken gold.
       Though words attempt portrayal of your eyes,
       My own observe that mere description lies.

You are, my love, refreshingly discreet,

It gives you no delight to wag your tongue;

You know how best the tongue and ear should meet

And such discretion keeps love ever young.

Longing to tell the world of your heart's flight,

Instead your secret shines within your face;

And from it love is radiating light,

Silently manifesting in your grace.

Burdening others never was your trait,

But should you need to speak about these things,

Just come to me with what you have to say

And we'll commune while joy, in silence, sings.

> For ere you speak of love, dear heart, know this –
>
> When you begin, I'll quiet you with a kiss.

I praise your beauty – you at once demur,

Yet flattery is not among my ways;

This you accept – but say you feel I err –

That faults dissolve beneath love's freeing gaze.

But is this so? I think we disagree:

What flaw could mar the patient face of love?

The beauty we on lovers' faces see

Is radiance from the heart, my gentle dove!

You know the world and men account you fair –

You need no fresh enhancement from my pen:

Yet just before I kiss you lying there,

I am impelled to say just once again:

    Though what is outside gratifies my sight,

    Know that your inward grace is my delight.

O do not say that time will quickly pass

As though your absence were a thing of naught;

Nor lightly speak of my impending fast

When I may taste you only in my thought.

To say that kisses now will stay me hence

O'erlooks what reason's prompting renders clear:

That feasts enjoyed long since and passed from sense

Will not give sustenance with no food near.

Men voyaging afar lay in great store,

Valuing now what has most future worth;

But how can I enjoy your presence more

And, by a gorging now, meet coming dearth?

     Yet when you journey, be it to a star,

     My ranging thoughts will find you where you are.

Why would my pen create again in time
With words, that dear perfection which you are,
As if in this I give you life in rhyme,
Unmindful that in falling short I mar?
Yet though my pen were still, you have two lives;
One as you are, the other in my heart.
That first is real and with your presence thrives –
The second I imagine when we part.
This double joy attends your comely charms,
I twice know love to see your lustrous eyes;
Those breasts, twin doves which nestle in your arms;
That dear twice-wrought perfection of your thighs.

    Duality in you gives joy to sight,
    But in your onenesses resides delight.

My love, were I the Lord of Time and Space

Who could command all things with form and name,

I'd keep you fast forever in this place,

And to our urgent need occasion frame.

For in your absence e'en the sunlight pales;

All that has lustre mutes its customed sheen.

Turning to thoughts for solace wholly fails;

The feast to come makes hunger now more keen.

Do not delight that I should feel this pain,

I can more fittingly devotion prove:

Rising to serve you here, I grow in vain,

Does not my plight your sweet compassion move?

    I must, it seems, resign myself to burn

    Until the quenching bliss of your return.

Some strands of hair have strayed across your face,

While in your eyes a cool excitement burns.

The sport of love is quickening its pace,

Your head, this way and that, restively turns;

The tiny beads of sweat which grace your brow

Glisten each time your face reflects the moon;

Those pearls (a present from the love-god) now

Must make requital as your senses swoon.

Breathless, you still find air for sighs' quick flight,

Ploughing my shoulders with your fiery nails,

Moaning a wordless language to the night,

Threshing beneath me as your spirit fails.

> Like quivering arrow centred in the mark,
>
> I fall upon you dying in the dark.

A subtle fragrance breathes about your hair,

Delighting sense yet mystifying quite.

What blend of substance makes a scent so rare,

Here in the vibrant stillness of the night?

You smell of earth when moistened by the rain,

Of waxy resin in the busy hive,

Of weathered cedar and of winnowed grain,

Or rain-washed hedgerows when the mayflowers thrive.

You smell of rushes, freshly gathered reeds,

Of woodland paths damp fragrant with decay;

Fine withered grasses, ripened nuts and seeds,

Of leather, timber, new-baked bread, and hay.

    Fragrant with mystery, moist with desire,

    Joying the senses with your quenching fire.

That which is sense now feels desire's command;

All that is tactile centres here in you.

The depths within you yield to my demand,

Our minds and spirits merge – were we once two?

Richly my senses feast on you their joy,

Drinking the beauty of your outer form;

Its sweet adroitness fully you deploy

Changing my inner state to mounting storm.

How tenderly you brook my fierce essay,

In ecstasy my soaring spirits fly!

Yet as you melt I can no longer stay,

The senses fuse – in paradise I die!

  Could Aphrodite so conclude love's rite?

  What has a goddess more, though she rule Night?

Watching you there reclining on the couch,

Radiant with beauty, peerless in your grace;

Seeing how what you feel your eyes avouch,

And that a smiling trust lights up your face;

It saddens me to think how Time's fell hand

Will soon with creases line your gentle brow;

And in the shadow of that flowing sand,

In silence, and unknown to you, I vow

That though the years must take their toll of you

Despite your wish to stay your youth for me,

Your selfless service, constant rich and true

Will mine command while life and breath agree.

    I love what lies within your outward form,

    And that time cannot mar nor age deform.

How is it that you seem for ever Spring,

While others of your kind feel pinch of years?

It seems the scythe of time will never bring

You down – no harvest of your charms yet nears.

Why does your offered richness never pall,

When even honey may the palate cloy?

For though you feast my senses, giving all,

Yet are you free of custom's dull annoy.

How has creation spared you youth's decline,

When even oceans suffer bated flow;

And do you make your favoured treasure mine,

That I through love this fortune too may know?

　　But why should all these questions answered be

　　When in your arms, the concept time will flee?

My love, the only time I've known you chafe

Is when I must at last rise from your arms.

Then as you lie, like some poor lonely waif

You gently pout as though I'd spurned your charms.

Yet all things measured, move toward their end

For nothing mortal 'scapes the flow of time;

And though like Circe you would apprehend,

I must ignore your sweet and tempting mime.

A river cannot always be in spate,

The sun itself retires for nightly rest;

Ardour, e'en mine, must for a while abate

If you would have love's vigour at its best.

    Then know that when your joy lies soft asleep,

    It rises, only tryst with you to keep.

You have about you that simplicity

Which gives the very young their special charm;

Yet you have womanhood in full degree

And, having both at once, you quite disarm.

Your company makes none of those demands

Which some might, with your beauty, claim as right;

And yet such excellence your grace commands

Your simplest acts at once express its light.

What you would have from me I long to give,

And you give all to me ere I require;

A rich exchange by which we grow and live,

Where those who give most, most acquire.

      Gently with love your presence nourishes;

      Within that light my spirit flourishes.

Love is a living concept all can know

Transcending any limits mind would frame;

And there are outward signs which lovers show

By which we recognise that we do name.

The lover is his substance outward poured,

And the beloved everywhere he sees;

He has no wish to limit the adored,

And by imposing no requirements, frees.

He gives, yet in that giving is entire,

For what is offered is received again;

And though much substance burns in love's sweet fire,

The wealth consumed yields undivided gain.

    As lovers offer more than ego's wealth,

    Each in return receives once more himself.

Will misty autumn ever cloud our years
Paling the sun that brightens youthful day?
Shall smiling fullness fade and melt in tears
And with a wintry frown incline away?
Seasons hold no sway in love's domain
Where reason plays its vital equal part;
The changing weather that gives rise to pain
Is kept where it belongs, within the heart.
Love has that rich eternal quality
Which does not waste with the expense of time;
And those who look from truth, as one, agree
That what is real is ever in its prime.
　　But love has poured such grace on you and me,
　　We are no test for this philosophy.

Love – A Cosmic Attractive Force

What ultimately is the concept Love

Which seems so much debased and misapplied?

Religions hint at origins above,

Though scientists such vaguenesses deride.

The absolute creative power expands

And, as creation, manifests itself;

The source, quite undiminished, ever stands

Unmoved, while movement demonstrates its wealth.

The causal power pervades what is expressed,

Exerting an attraction for the source;

What flows, is back towards itself addressed,

Drawn self-ward by its own inhering force.

    As substance by its gravity attracts,

    We see how love within creation acts.

The Care of Instinct

When man, endowed with reason, moves to act,
His finer judgement balances his deeds;
And he may well, impelled by love, contract
That which his own self-interest impedes.

But animals not so endowed, require
An ineluctable unerring care
To meet their needs; where absence of desire
Is met by drives, and error will be rare.

Each creature in vast evolution's range
Instinctively, its sure direction draws
As it responds adaptively to change,
Within the stern support of Nature's laws.

    Men's bodies too are by this instinct ruled,
    But minds by reason, hearts by love, are schooled.

Love's Origin

The fundamental principle of Love
Stems from the Absolute, sole origin
Of all that is beloved. For as the glove
Takes life and movement from the hand within,
So the Creator, in the act itself,
Is that creation and its very life;
And all the turning splendour, all the wealth
Of change is the Creator's glory – rife.
Distinction and variety converge
In the belovèd who, reflecting One,
Intensifies the urgent will to merge
And, in the way of Love, the prize is won.

    So lovers merge their twin identity
    Releasing spirit in their unity.

To a Dark Lady

At my life's edge I heard a rustling gown
And glancing up, beheld your patient eyes
Which long had waited for that look, look down;
And, stirred within my soul, felt love arise.
I saw a radiance, beauty fresh as Spring,
Your dark hair burnished like a sable sun;
Your silk gown swirling like liquid flowing
About you as you moved, majestic one!
My breath quickens with your breast's rise and fall;
Do you move, unaware how you move me?
How can these cyphers – words – convey that all
Which is your self, that living poetry?
      If none are perfect who must breathe the air,
      O grant such imperfection everywhere!

Borne by your presence like a sound in air

Floats fragrance of the finest essences

Distilled by the perfumer; made rarer

As your peerless alchemy advances

Love's cause, and you my inner spaces fill.

For when you leave each place which you enhance,

Your trace upon the ambience lingers still;

Beyond remembered sound and parting glance.

Your presence, which delights the heart and mind,

Is joyous subject of my senses' play;

And in this resonance, we two aligned

As one, find love content with us to stay.

    Your every movement in caressing air

    Leaves on the sense your spirit's fragrance there.

The living depths which light your lovely eyes
Grow deeper with increased proximity;
And as I move, your nearness magnifies
The rich enchantment of immediacy.
As admiration brings preparedness
For giving to exceed received delight,
The joyous presence of your eagerness
Proclaims attunement standing at the height.
Your fragrance penetrates the mind like sound,
A subtle invitation finely sung;
The sense of touch felicity has found
In mute caressing converse, tongue to tongue.
  Our very souls near union in this
  The full commingling of a searching kiss.

Knowing your beauty has enchanted me

But that my eyes see so much more than this,

Why do you disallow instinctively

The voicing of my love – yet let me kiss?

O hear again as I profession make

With candour rare in words which lovers cast;

Grant that I may of you some easement take

If my avowal win your heart at last.

Should wanting you proclaim my selfishness

The fault is mine, your merit is the reason;

But let devotion show my selflessness –

Its time is now and evermore its season.

    That I love you, you know that it is so;

    And that you'd hear it, hear it, this I know.

How many hours we two have whiled away,

For which a sterner man might censure us?

Yet two in love who spend a careless day

Will gain, at zealous times, fresh stimulus.

The trees which idle in their winter rime

Stand waiting for the lively call of Spring;

Their indolent display at blossom time

A vital preface to their harvesting.

Such richness permeates your industry,

It fires the earnestness with which you give;

The flowing measure of your love for me

Ordains the ambience in which I live.

    Which said, who now will strictly count the hours

    Of seeming lightness in which loving flowers?

I'll not forbear to press your gentle limbs

From fear my weight might bruise their gentleness;

For never yet did bee, where nectar brims,

Not burden blossom with its soft impress.

Dear one, the wakeful moon is shining still,

Why is it you desire again to rest?

Stay not to slumber, precious hours o'erspill;

This night the sightless love god is our guest.

Let us not sleep 'till velvet night is gone,

And moonbeams pale before the rising sun;

When morning light is your caparison

Then is the time to think our loving done.

    For youth departs, occasion slips away;

    Let us not rue a wasted yesterday!

My love, at last your eyelids close in sleep,

Yet still your face outshines the radiant moon;

With night far spent, I too can scarcely keep

Awake and sleep will claim us both ere soon.

The god of love smiles at your disarray,

Seeing your lovely hair in tangled tresses;

And he or I will kiss all trace away

If I too ardently gave my caresses.

The marks upon your neck will quickly fade,

As will the imprints on your ear above.

Now, separating sleep waits to invade

Our limbs all drowsy with the spells of love;

     Some last endearments whispered in the night,

     And sleep dissolves the images of sight.

Your lovely presence sweeps away all doubt,

In those who wondered if you could be real;

As though my inspiration were without

Your substance – an imagined, dreamt ideal.

How many people daily pass you by

And travel on unmoved? Incredibly

The same rich world greets every person's eye,

Yet some its subtler beauties never see.

Abundant glimpses of you intersperse

These lines, a fact you never once have claimed;

You have occasioned and inspired my verse,

And breathe it through, although you are not named.

  You, love, are no delusive ecstasy

  But a delightful, warm, responsive she.

You have, my love, sparked thought from wisdom's source;
The whole creation is resolved to three!
We both, with love, make up the triple force
That constitutes our lively galaxy.
With cosmic chemistry in your embrace,
Light in the simple candour of your heart,
Your presence is the spirit's dwelling place
Wherein a new creative act may start.
As that intense consummate moment nears,
Yielding its timeless manifest of troth,
That melting comes, when either disappears,
When separateness dissolves and each is both.
    Self meets itself in ultimate address,
    Receiving blissful joy in consciousness.

To Time – A Plea for Consistency

A double standard ill becomes thy years,

And gravest consequences could ensue

If, obdurate, thou closest up thine ears;

For this in brief is our complaint and rue;

Thou tripp'st it pertly when with her I stay

And all too soon thine hour-glass sand is sped,

But when we wait before some special day,

Old tardy one, thou creep'st on feet of lead.

Dost thou my lady's power to charm decline

Because thou saw'st fair Helen long ago,

And heard the lovely Sappho speak a rhyme?

Old man these maids are dead, mine liveth now!

    We ask no favours from thine ancient hand;

    Be thou but even when thou runn'st thy sand.

To the Goddess of Love

O Aphrodite, in whose perfect grace
The concept love is giv'n immortal guise;
Who, though divine, reveal'st to men thy face
In glimpses mirrored from a lover's eyes.
Thy benediction like a mantle sits
In rich attendance on my earthly sight
As grace an audience of thyself permits,
Piercing this veil of flesh with love's clear light.
A maiden breathes (one surely known to thee)
Who hath love's measure full within her heart.
This angel might thine own sweet minion be,
So nobly hath she ta'en the woman's part.
 For though 'tis true a mortal form she bears,
 Divinely she her human habit wears.

A Reproof to Cupid

Young wayward marksman, lay aside thy bow:

Such sport as thou hast had is not a game.

Wert thou not blind, by now thou'd surely know

Those misplaced arrows sorely wound and maim.

Our tender girls to lose their treasure strive

And powerful men yield sovereignty to maids;

Thy goddess mother and Adonis thrive,

But others find love's pleasure slowly fades.

Such ill-assorted pairings have occurred

That wounded harts and hinds in wedded thorn –

According to reports which I have heard –

Regard all thoughts of love with blatant scorn.

    Whether we blame thy fletcher or thine aim,

    'Tis clear thy tricks have sullied love's good name.

Helen of Troy

What had this face that launched a thousand ships
More than so many others without flaw?
What quality had Helen's breasts and hips
To merit, first abduction, then a war!
Captured by Theseus, at the age of ten;
Later on, beseiged by all those suitors;
Did more than beauty fascinate these men –
Acquired allure, learned from skilful tutors?
Was she endowed with more than other maids,
Or just adroitly managed and arranged?
While captive during Troy's great siege and raids,
Was she entirely from love's joys estranged?
     But this must cease, this trial in retrospect;
     A legend's beauty should be shown respect!

Notes

1 In 1953 James Watson and Francis Crick worked out the structure of DNA and postulated the now famous double helix model. The main structural element in this molecular arrangement comprises sugar and phosphate groups. Attached to the sugar molecule is one of four possible bases which, because of this variation, can represent information. Occasional 'misprints' occur as replication takes place but the miraculous language, which can frame an amoeba and an elephant within the same grammar, is amazingly consistent.

2 Haiku are rather more than succinct verses of poetry; they are visionary moments expressed with economy and objectivity. In the Japanese they contain seventeen syllables and any translation is but a shadow, which can do no more than suggest the original. The haiku, which R H Blyth has described as an 'artistic asceticism', has a long history. Its terseness and immediacy give it a great deal in common with Zen and a study of this relationship is revealing. No single haiku could be typical of a form capable of such variety, but if one is to serve as an example, let it be the famous verse by Bashō:

> An old pond;
> A frog jumps in –
> The sound of water!

3 For the ancient Greeks the Kore was an important monumental art form which evolved over 200 years. These sculptures of a standing maiden, usually in marble, developed from a severe figure to a naturalistic, though idealized, representation of great beauty. Between 650 BC and c480 BC, the figure gradually relaxed from a rigid posture 'at attention' to an easier stance, sometimes taking a step forward with arms away from the sides. The hair and clothing became more natural, and sometimes pigment was used to obtain greater realism. Faces softened and the haunting trace of a smile appeared.

4 In a classical Sanskrit text of aesthetic theory, (the *Nātyashāstra* of Bharata), eight 'Permanent Emotional Modes' are listed. In Bharata's sequence the first, 'Delight' and its flavour the erotic, is usually regarded as the highest in significance. This is because it lies closest to the bliss of religious enlightenment, which is a universal self-transcendent feeling analagous to the supreme bliss of ultimate release from birth and death. Eroticism ranks as a science in India and the sexual act represents union between Essence and Substance.

The sculptures in many of the temples at Khajuraho, like the architecture, show particular refinement. The frank naiveté sometimes seen at Konarak does not appear, and one is inclined to the view that obscenity, like beauty, is in the eye of the beholder.

5 The word Tao (pronounced 'Dow') has no single apt translation. Its meaning is beyond words even in the Chinese language. Great Chinese writings, particularly the *Tao-Te-Ching* and the *Chuang-Tzu*, contain collections of sayings, stories and allegories which allude to it but do not define it.

> 'The Supreme Tao is formless, yet It produces and nurtures Heaven and Earth.
> The Supreme Tao has no desires, yet by Its power the Sun and Moon revolve
>   in their orbits.
> The Supreme Tao is nameless, yet It ever supports all things.
> I do not know Its name but for title, call It Tao.'

> 'The Tao that can be told is not the eternal Tao.
> The name that can be named is not the eternal name.
> The nameless is the beginning of heaven and earth.
> The named is the mother of ten thousand things.'

Two of the great intuitions of Tao are:

> Nothing that happens ever exactly repeats itself.
> This immense web of continual change does not itself change.

6 Jalal al-Din Rūmī (1207-1273) was born at Khorasan in the most north-eastern province of Persia. Generally regarded as the greatest of the Persian mystical poets, his output was as prodigious as it was sublime in content.

He wrote some 2,500 mystical odes in the composition known as *Diwani Shamsi Tabriz*;

The *Mathnawī* containing some 25,000 rhyming couplets;

The *Ruba'Iyat* which has about 1,600 quatrains.

Rūmī is said to have founded the Mevlevi Order of Whirling Dervishes at Konya in Turkey, whose ceremony of circling configuration opens the mind to an understanding of the Natural Order in creation. At the culmination of the all-night turning ceremonies, Rūmī would instruct his followers by means of verses, parables and conversations. The Persian reed-flute (ney) features prominently in the religious ceremonies of the Mevlevi, with the emphasis on music and sacred dancing. In the opening lines of the Mathnawī, the great poet uses the reed to symbolize the soul emptied of self (ego) and filled with the Divine spirit. Remembering its earlier union with God it yearns for release from this world in which it is a stranger in exile.

7 Utamaro is one of a number of Japanese artists now deservedly receiving recognition in the West. He was born in 1753 at Edo where he lived until his death in 1788, and where he was a key figure in a thriving culture. He painted in the style known as Ukiyo-e (the Floating World) which by then was fully developed, as was colour-printing, having been introduced in the early 17th century. The 'Floating World' artists, as they were called, often took as their subjects the courtesans and escorts who frequented the tea-houses and pleasure gardens of Edo, sometimes depicting them in boating parties on, or by, the Sumida River. Utamaro's best broadsheets have an eloquent charm, which, together with their fine composition and sureness of line, mark him out from most others in the colour-print movement.

Besides his colour prints and brush paintings, Utamaro illustrated three renowned and beautiful books of birds, insects and shells. As an illustrator his imaginative designs and technical brilliance have seldom been equalled.

Index of First Lines